D1222670

Animals of Africa

LIONS

by Mary Meinking

FOCUS
READERS

www.focusreaders.com

Focus Readers is distributed by North Star Editions:
sales@northstareditions.com | 888-417-0195

Produced for Focus Readers by Red Line Editorial.

Photographs ©: Maggy Meyer/Shutterstock Images, cover, 1, 4–5, 8; Red Line Editorial, 6; squashedbox/iStockphoto, 7; Oleg Znamenskiy/Shutterstock Images, 10–11; skynesher/ iStockphoto, 12; Edwin Butter/Shutterstock Images, 14–15; WLDavies/iStock, 16–17, 22–23, 26 (top); Eric Isselee/Shutterstock Images, 18; JacoBecker/Shutterstock Images, 20; LyleGregg/iStockphoto, 24; AndreAnita/iStockphoto, 26 (bottom right); Stuart G Porter/ Shutterstock Images, 26 (bottom left); MogensTrolle/iStockphoto, 27

ISBN
978-1-63517-266-9 (hardcover)
978-1-63517-331-4 (paperback)
978-1-63517-461-8 (ebook pdf)
978-1-63517-396-3 (hosted ebook)

Library of Congress Control Number: 2017935123

Printed in the United States of America
Mankato, MN
June, 2017

About the Author

Mary Meinking works as a graphic designer during the day. In her spare time, she has written more than 30 children's books. Topics include history, arts and crafts, extreme jobs, animals, pop stars, and travel. When not working, writing, or hanging out with her family in Iowa, Mary enjoys doing crafts, photography, baking, and traveling.

TABLE OF CONTENTS

CHAPTER 1

PRIDE LAND

It is a hot day. Some lions lie on rocks. Others find shade. Male lions guard their **territory**. The lionesses care for the young. In the evening, these females will hunt. For now, the lions rest.

 Rocks are a cool place for lions to rest.

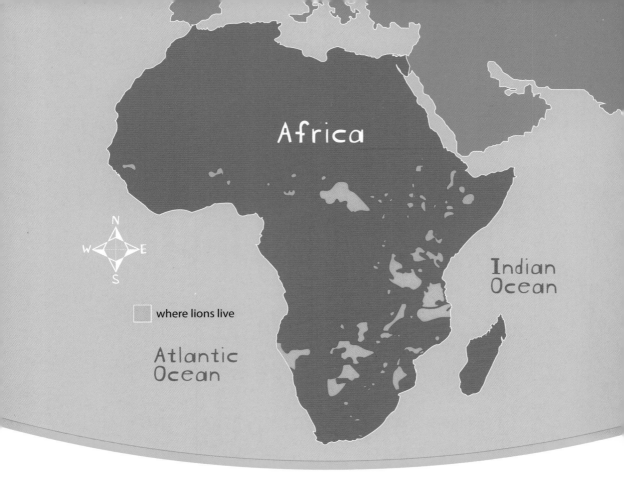

Africa

N
W   E
S

Indian
Ocean

 where lions live

Atlantic
Ocean

> **Lions live in many areas of Africa.**

Lions live in Africa. Many are
found in the Serengeti National
Park. They often live in open
grasslands. They can also live in

 The dark tip of a lion's tail stands out against the grass.

swampy areas. Others make their

homes in thick woods or **scrub**

forests. Lions hide in tall grass

while hunting their **prey**.

 A male lion watches over its territory.

A lion's territory is hot and dry. There are not many trees. The lions find cool places to rest. Some lions nap in trees.

Each male lion protects a territory. It can cover 100 square miles (259 sq. km). The male lion patrols its area. It watches carefully for intruders.

CHAPTER 2

MANE EVENT

Lions are large **predators**. Adult males weigh more than 400 pounds (180 kg). That makes them bigger than a couch. Adult lionesses weigh approximately 280 pounds (127 kg).

A female lion (front) is smaller than a male lion.

 Only male lions have manes.

Lions are covered in tan fur. They have pads on the bottom of their feet. These pads are also surrounded by fur. The fur silences their steps.

Male lions are known for their thick **manes**. These manes make lions look bigger. As a male lion gets older, his mane darkens.

Lions have long, thin tails. The tails have dark tufts of fur at the end. Lions use their tails to balance. The dark tip helps them follow one another in tall grass.

FUN FACT

Male lions are the only cats that have manes.

WHITE LIONS

Not all lions are tan. A few are white. Instead of golden eyes, their eyes are green or blue. But they act and hunt like their tan relatives.

Some white lions were captured and put in zoos. Others were hunted for their unusual coats. By 1994, no white lions were left in the wild.

But in 2004, three white lion **prides** were put back into the wild. They live in a nature **preserve**. No hunters are allowed there. Today, white lion cubs are again born in the wild.

This white lion lives at a zoo.

CHAPTER 3

TOOTH AND CLAW

A lion is built to hunt. Every part of its body works together to capture prey. A lion's tan coat is the same color as the grass around it. It blends into its surrounding. This helps the lion sneak up on its prey.

 A lioness walks through the grass in search of prey.

PARTS OF A LION

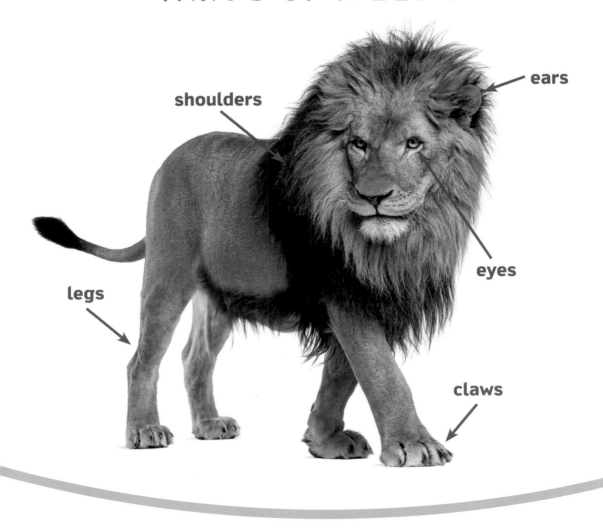

shoulders

ears

eyes

legs

claws

Female lions are quicker than males. This helps them catch prey more easily.

Lions often hunt at night. They use their senses to track prey. Their **pupils** are large. This helps lions see at night. A lion can also hear prey more than 1 mile (1.6 km) away. The lion turns each ear in a different direction. This helps the lion hear sounds from all around.

FUN FACT

Lions have loose belly skin. This helps protect their insides if they are kicked by prey.

A lion has 30 sharp teeth.

A lion is muscular. It has strong
shoulders. A lion can hold down
an animal three times larger than

itself. A lion's leg muscles help it quickly pounce and capture its prey.

Lions have razor-sharp teeth. The teeth can slice through flesh. A lion's tongue is rough like sandpaper. A lion uses its tongue to peel skin off prey. The tongue also scrapes meat off bones.

Hook-like claws help lions climb. Lions also use their claws to defend themselves and grab prey. A lion's claws **retract** when not needed.

CHAPTER 4

LION'S SHARE

Lions live in family groups called prides. A pride has at least one adult male. It also includes several adult females. A pride can have dozens of young lions, too. The young are called cubs.

 A pride of lions walks through its territory.

Two cubs play near their mother.

The females in a pride are related. They stay together for life. Females usually have two to four cubs at a time. Cubs start eating meat when they are three months old. They hunt at a year old. The pride hunts and guards its territory together. All pride members help raise the cubs. Adults work together to care for the cubs. Female lions often live up to 16 years in the wild. But males rarely live longer than 12 years.

LION LIFE CYCLE

It is common for females to have two to four cubs.

Lions hunt when they are one year old.

Adult lions guard their territory.

 A lioness chases a zebra.

Lions are **carnivores**. The females do most of the hunting. They work together to surround and attack their prey. Lions often eat gazelles or zebras. They can eat up to 60 pounds (27 kg) of meat at each meal.

FOCUS ON
LIONS

Write your answers on a separate sheet of paper.

1. Write a sentence that describes the key ideas from Chapter 3.

2. Would you like to see a lion in real life? Why or why not?

3. Which lions do most of the hunting?
   A. cubs
   B. males
   C. females

4. How does a lion's tan fur help it catch prey?
   A. The prey stops running because it is afraid of the lion's color.
   B. The prey doesn't see the lion because its fur blends in with the grass.
   C. The lion can run faster because of the color of its fur.

5. What does **raise** mean in this book?

*All pride members help **raise** the cubs. Adults work together to care for the cubs.*

    A. to lift something up
    B. to fight an enemy
    C. to feed and protect

6. What does **pounce** mean in this book?

*A lion's leg muscles help it quickly **pounce** and capture its prey.*

    A. to eat prey
    B. to suddenly jump
       on prey
    C. to run a long distance

Answers on page 32.

GLOSSARY

carnivores
Animals that eat meat.

manes
The hair that grows on the necks of some animals.

predators
Animals that hunt other animals for food.

preserve
An area of land set aside for managing and protecting animals.

prey
An animal that is hunted and killed by another animal for food.

prides
Groups of lions.

pupils
The dark centers of the eye that allow light to enter.

retract
To pull in claws.

scrub
An area of land covered in bushes or shrubs.

territory
An area that is defended by a group of animals.

TO LEARN MORE

BOOKS

Joubert, Bethany, and Dereck Joubert. *Face to Face with Lions*. Washington, DC: National Geographic Children's Books, 2010.

Meinking, Mary. *Lion vs. Gazelle.* Chicago: Heinemann-Raintree, 2011.

Owings, Lisa. *The African Lion.* Hopkins, MN: Bellwether Media, 2012.

NOTE TO EDUCATORS

Visit **www.focusreaders.com** to find lesson plans, activities, links, and other resources related to this title.

INDEX

Answer Key: 1. Answers will vary; 2. Answers will vary; 3. C; 4. B; 5. C; 6. B